MOTION LEADERSHIP

MICHAEL FULLAN

MOTION LEADERSHIP

THE SKINNY
on Becoming Change Savvy

A JOINT PUBLICATION

CORWIN
A SAGE Company

OPC
ONTARIO PRINCIPALS' COUNCIL

SCHOOL IMPROVEMENT NETWORK.

AASA
AMERICAN ASSOCIATION OF SCHOOL ADMINISTRATORS

learningforward

For information:

Corwin
A SAGE Company
2455 Teller Road
Thousand Oaks, California 91320
(800) 233-9936
Fax: (800) 417-2466
www.corwinpress.com

SAGE India Pvt. Ltd.
B 1/I 1 Mohan Cooperative Industrial Area
Mathura Road, New Delhi 110 044
India

SAGE Ltd.
1 Oliver's Yard
55 City Road
London EC1Y 1SP
United Kingdom

SAGE Asia-Pacific Pte. Ltd.
33 Pekin Street #02-01
Far East Square
Singapore 048763

Printed in the United States of America

Library of Congress Cataloging-in-Publication Data

Fullan, Michael.
Motion leadership: The skinny on becoming change savvy/Michael Fullan.
p. cm.
Includes bibliographical references and index.
ISBN 978-1-4129-8131-6 (pbk.)
1. Educational leadership. 2. Educational change. I. Title.

LB2806.F796 2010
371.2—dc22 2009033906

This book is printed on acid-free paper.

10 11 12 13 10 9 8 7 6 5 4

Acquisitions Editor: Arnis Burvikovs
Associate Editor: Desirée A. Bartlett
Editorial Assistants: Joanna Coelho and Kimberly Greenberg
Production Editor: Melanie Birdsall
Copy Editor: Adam Dunham
Typesetter: C&M Digitals (P) Ltd.
Proofreader: Cheryl Rivard
Indexer: Sheila Bodell
Cover Designer: Scott Van Atta

CONTENTS

ABOUT THE AUTHOR

Michael Fullan is professor emeritus of the Ontario Institute for Studies in Education of the University of Toronto. Recognized as a worldwide authority on educational reform, Fullan is engaged in training, consulting, and evaluating change projects around the world, and his books have been published in many languages.

Fullan is currently Special Advisor to the Premier and Minister of Education in Ontario. His book *Leading in a Culture of Change* was awarded the 2002 Book of the Year Award by Learning Forward (formerly the National Staff Development Council), and *Breakthrough* (with Peter Hill and Carmel Crévola) won the 2006 Book of the Year Award from the American Association of Colleges for Teacher Education. His latest books are *The Six Secrets of Change* (Jossey-Bass), *What's Worth Fighting For in the Principalship* (Teachers College Press), and (with Geoff Scott) *Turnaround Leadership in Higher Education* (Jossey-Bass).

Among his Corwin titles are *Realization: The Change Imperative for Deepening District-Wide Reform* (with Lyn Sharratt), *Breakthrough* (with Peter Hill and Carmel Crévola), *Leadership & Sustainability: System Thinkers in Action,* the second edition of

The Challenge of Change: Start School Improvement Now! and the new *All Systems Go*.

A list of his widely acclaimed books, articles, and other resources can be found at www.michaelfullan.ca.

CHAPTER ONE
THE SKINNY

We were standing outside Queen Elizabeth Conference Center in London in May 2009, after our 100th or so daylong workshop in the past year—this time with 200 school and district leaders from four local boroughs. Claudia Cuttress, my manager; Alan Boyle, our U.K. and Ireland agent; and I began to discuss life beyond the workshop. As we looked up at Big Ben and took in the Westminster aura, we talked about the limitations of conducting session after session, day after day. As successful as these workshops were in terms of participant ratings (usually 4.6 on a 5-point scale), the impact did not seem to add up ("You can't workshop the world!").

Books were fine at spreading the ideas at an awareness level, but how could we reach more people in a deeper fashion? Making a DVD did not seem to be the answer either—just another passive medium. We had flirted over the years with online production but were never satisfied with either the quality of video technology or the pedagogical design and depth. But now we knew that technology was no longer an issue—we used increasingly high-quality and sophisticated technology in our workshops.

> "You can't workshop the world!"

So we revisited the online question and within five minutes came up with the concept we wanted—*Motion Leadership.* It seemed like no one of us had the idea. It was as if we mouthed it simultaneously. What we were doing in our work was helping leaders "move" individuals, institutions, and whole systems forward. We knew a great deal about positive motion and how to deal with the frustrations of lack of movement. We then began to discuss the notion of how to build a series of movielike experiences that could be accessed online with dynamic footage and tools to help any leader move forward. We call this *Motion Leadership the Movie* (MLM)—a product that will be available in 2010. It is not a movie in the Hollywood sense, but rather uses motion, visuals, video streams, tools, instruments, and ideas to bring change alive and enable the participant to become immersed in action. We want to capture in a multisensory way what it means and what it feels like to "move" forward in a way that excites and motivates people.

What we have written here is not MLM but its precursor. It contains basic ideas and insights about change. We call it the *skinny* on change savvy. "What's the skinny on change" perfectly fits what we want to convey. This is an expression that apparently arose in World War II when a leader demanded "the skinny naked truth." Literally, *the skinny* is about the naked unadorned facts—the core unobscured essence of the matter. The skinny on *Motion Leadership* change can be best expressed around eight elements: change problems, change itself, connecting peers with purpose, capacity building trumps judgmentalism, learning is the work, transparency rules, love, trust and resistance, and leadership for all.

What we were doing in our work was helping leaders "move" individuals, institutions, and whole systems forward.

How complex is bringing about positive change on a large scale? Damn so—judging from the history of failed attempts over the past half century. Getting at the skinny is to make change less complex and more powerful in its impact. Let's use the Food Channel as an example because we will be focusing along the way on Jamie Oliver. Being able to prepare good and great food consistently used to be extremely complex. If you went to the recipes of the great French chefs, you could get lost in the sauces by the time you got to step three (not to mention that you needed a whole day to do the preparation). Or anyone who has seen an Italian mama at work in the kitchen will marvel at the outcome—and at the fact that nothing seems to be written down. What the Food Network has done is to get to the skinny (no pun intended) of good cooking. These days, anyone—with a little persistent effort—can become a very good cook. The complex has become simple while the result has dramatically improved—a perfect recipe for powerful change.

> *The skinny* is about the naked unadorned facts—the core unobscured essence of the matter.

Jeff Kluger (2008) was getting at this phenomenon in his book *Simplexity: Why Simple Things Become Complex (and How Complex Things Can Be Made Simple).* He shows, for example, how we pursue too many targets including many of the wrong ones, how we fail to come up with a clear sense of where to focus our efforts, how governments waste money on the wrong strategies, and so on (a warning though—you won't get the skinny on motion change in *Simplexity*).

> Getting at the skinny is to make change less complex and more powerful in its impact.

The skinny boils down and names the key insights that leaders need to know about understanding and working with change.

Reading this booklet will increase your knowledge and insight about change but not your skills and competencies. For the latter, you need also to learn about action ideas from other practitioners, apply them in your own situation, and debrief in order to keep on learning. MLM is designed so that people can build skills and competencies as they work with the insights. Our whole effort is not about discussing change but about getting into it. It is a "let's get going" proposition in which insights and strategies are going to have the appearance of simplicity while at the same time unleashing powerful and in many ways marvelously complex processes. The skinny takes the mystery out of complexity.

> The complex has become simple while the result has dramatically improved—a perfect recipe for powerful change.

It is revealing to observe that our practical theory was not developed out of research and then applied. Indeed, the opposite is closer to the truth. We tried to bring about positive change in larger and larger settings—classrooms, schools, districts, whole states, provinces, and countries. We also brought motion leadership to the big arena—how to make "all systems go," in which system leaders cause positive motion of the whole system, achieving remarkable results (Fullan, 2010).

> Our whole effort is not about discussing change but about getting into it.

What we learned along the way has made the theories stronger and sharper. Stated another way, we moved from practice to theory with ever increasing refinement. In fact, my personal indicator of whether we are being successful is when scores of practitioners using the ideas come to internalize them in a way that they can articulate the theory of action better than the best academics—something you will see in MLM as practitioners illustrate and talk about how they get positive motion.

Our team in one sense is very large. There is a small core of regulars, but also a larger set of people who mix and match on applied projects around the world. In addition to Claudia and Alan, Joanne Quinn and Eleanor Adam are master capacity-building designers and deliverers. Nancy Watson is a great critical decipherer, analyst, and writer. The "Saint," Clif Saint Germain, is a deeply committed and skilled change agent on the ground. Bill Hogarth and Lyn Sharratt are able to lead the transformation of a very large urban school district. Peter Hill and Carmel Crévola are the best policy-practice duo anywhere. Carol Rolheiser, Professor Pedagogy Plus, is leading the improvement of teaching across the University of Toronto with over 50,000 students, faculty, and teaching assistants.

In the big policy and political picture there is Ben Levin, variously fabulous deputy minister and academic; leadership guru Ken Leithwood; Sir Michael Barber, the globe-trotting transformer of the systems; Tony Mackay, one of the world's best facilitators (call him "Motion Mackay"); David Hopkins, equally skilled at mountain climbing and change agency; Andy Hargreaves, brother in arms, always incisive; and even a politician, premier Dalton McGuinty, the best education premier anywhere. And it is not just K–12 education. More recently, we have linked forces with Charles Pascal in Ontario on early learning and Geoff Scott in Australia on the small matter of turning around higher education.

What all of us have in common is the moral commitment and ongoing immersion in addressing real change problems, striving for positive impact. It is all large scale. Not a few schools here and there,

> We moved from practice to theory with ever increasing refinement.

but whole districts, whole states, whole countries. If it sounds exciting, it is. But it is also humbling. None of us for a moment think we can bring about change in the next situation without partnering with hordes of others—teaming up to work through the vicissitudes of each new culture. We go by Pfeffer and Sutton's (2008) definition of wisdom, "the ability to act with knowledge while doubting what you know" (p. 174). You get smarter, but you are also more acutely aware of what you don't know.

In *Motion Leadership,* we have also partnered with two entrepreneurial organizations who themselves have joined up for this purpose: Corwin and the School Improvement Network (SINet). It is a dream to work with Leigh Peake, the dynamic new president of Corwin; the streetwise editor Arnis Burvikovs; and Curtis Linton, the creative vice president of SINet—all committed to pushing the frontiers of online motion learning. Curtis trekked over to England on the spur of the moment to film our workshops in London and Derby in order to get a personal feel for the nature of the work and its possibilities.

> None of us for a moment think we can bring about change in the next situation without partnering with hordes of others—teaming up to work through the vicissitudes of each new culture.

When MLM is completed, it will feature named situations and people as they grapple with motion leadership. We will see change through their eyes as well as through the filter of what we know about how change does move successfully. Our goal with MLM—a movie supplemented with interactive tools and other supports—is to get people immersed in "real change," their own and others' change situations. The notion is to create an experience that is tantamount to watching and being in a movie at the same time.

> Our goal with MLM—a movie supplemented with interactive tools and other supports—is to get people immersed in "real change," their own and others' change situations.

In the meantime, the skinny is designed so that it can be read on its own. It is a stand-alone book. It gives the essentials about change knowledge, intending to be practically insightful. We hope that reading this short book will further your basic change knowledge in a way that helps you grapple with change situations right away. For those who wish to become more immersed, and to work on developing the knowledge, skills, and dispositions of becoming change savvy, MLM is intended to be a deeper experiential source of learning, led in many ways by practitioners.

One more thing about the skinny: to master it is to accelerate the speed of quality change. Effective change cannot be accomplished overnight, but skinny change agents can accomplish quality implementation with high impact in remarkable short time frames—much shorter than we hitherto thought possible.

So, jump onboard. We are going to take you on a journey. No need to bring your trunks. We are going "skinny dipping."

CHAPTER TWO

CHANGE PROBLEMS

Change problems come in all shapes and sizes, but they all have one thing in common—they are mired in inertia. The goal of all change leaders in these situations is to get movement in an improved direction. Motion leadership causes great new things to happen.

Bill Hogarth, the director of education in the York Region District School Board, faced the inertia of the status quo when, as a new CEO in 1999, he stunned the system when he said that all York children should be reading by the end of kindergarten. Mobilizing 9,000 teachers and 130,000 students in 190 schools is no mean change feat.

> Motion leadership causes great new things to happen.

Courtney Millet, superintendent of St. John the Baptist Parish just outside New Orleans, has only 13 schools, but the inertia of the past is even more deeply entrenched. The district has had the same top-heavy central structure for over 100 years. She and her colleagues must figure out how to create a more visible presence in the schools in order to help students with minimal prior learning to become literate.

Or how about Jamie Oliver, the young high-profile chef in London, who was appalled when he saw the food being served every day in schools. In examining some of the dishes, he was unable to discern any of the ingredients. Maybe not a recipe for scurvy, but certainly for obesity and multiple health problems that affected children's energy and capacity to focus on their learning. He set out to change the eating habits of children in one school only to face an army of stalwarts of the status quo from the "head dinner lady" and her staff to the kids themselves who revolted at Jamie's food, to the parents who smuggled through the school fence a poor diet of fatty processed food to their children in order to subvert the new food regime.

Eventually, after enormous effort, experiencing some success in this one school, Jamie realized that his victory means nothing on such a small scale. So he decided to take on the whole borough of Greenwich with its 60 schools. What kind of change savvy did he need to turn 60 head dinner ladies into change agents? We will hear more about his journey in subsequent chapters.

Perhaps you are a principal of one of Ontario's "Schools on the Move," some 150 elementary schools that have demonstrated three successive years of improvement in literacy and numeracy. Can you explain to others what you did that caused the improvements much less help other school leaders who, as part of the Ontario strategy, want to learn from you?

You could be a school or district leader in Ontario's Huron Perth Catholic District School Board. Similar to St. John the Baptist only in the number of schools (18), Huron Perth has moved from being an adequate school district to a very good one. How do you sustain these gains, maintain momentum, and move from good to great? How can you go deeper and sustain the energy and improvements across the whole system?

> How do you sustain these gains, maintain momentum, and move from good to great? How can you go deeper and sustain the energy and improvements across the whole system?

What if you were Dalton McGuinty, premier of Ontario, and had presented yourself in 2003 as the education premier, vowing to take the stagnant public education system of some 5,000 schools to new heights? And what if you accomplished a great deal of this by 2009 and wondered how you could do more, much more, in the two years you have left in your current mandate in a bid to leave a legacy of lasting change?

Then there is Sallyann Stanton, a newly appointed grade-level leader in Southampton, England, expected to lead a group of more experienced teachers whose informal leader is a science teacher who makes it clear that she has no use for any new ways. What kind of change savvy did Sallyann need to form a positive moving relationship with this teacher and her group? She did it by using motion leadership ideas. In sequence, she first empathized and listened. She then involved the teacher in a task that she was good at—a small-scale effort. As Sallyann moved closer to action, she told the group that she would first try out the new ideas and would take responsibility if they failed. Being change savvy, she knew that "taking the fear out of change" is key. Sallyann was consciously building relationships over time with the group and the individuals in it. And only after establishing some rapport did she step up the challenges for the group to go further. Sallyann is humble (I don't have all the answers), while simultaneously

> She told the group that she would first try out the new ideas and would take responsibility if they failed. Being change savvy, she knew that "taking the fear out of change" is key.

pressing hard for more change. Sallyann is now the head of Kanes Hill primary school in Southampton, building on her change knowledge and getting more improvements than ever.

Imagine that it is 1990, and you are the director of education or a school head in the newly formed London Borough of Tower Hamlets. Up until 1990, you had been part of the Inner London Education Authority (ILEA), the largest district in Europe encompassing 12 boroughs and over 60,000 teachers. Now, thanks to Margaret Thatcher, you are part of the dismantling process and have your own local autonomy. Tower Hamlets lies east of the city of London on the north bank of the river Thames. Its historic name originated in the 16th century when the inhabitants in the area were required to furnish the yeomen for the Tower of London, which remains in the borough at its western edge. What if someone told you in 1990 that by 2009 (and much sooner), you would have been part of a coordinated leadership collective that made Tower Hamlets, with its 97 schools and 37,500 pupils, the fastest- and best-improving local authority in England—despite having the highest unemployment rate, and with 52% of the population being very poor Bangladeshi immigrants? Definitely a case of motion leadership, but how did they do it? In later chapters, we will draw on Alan Boyle's account to show how this was done, including the role of the intriguing new concept of "collaborative competition."

What would you do if you were Wendy Thomson, the new chief executive of Newham Council, a very large municipality in England, who spent a full year conducting forums of discussion about a new vision, talking to thousands of people—only to find, from a survey, after 12 months that 80% of the people had never heard of the vision; and of the remaining 20%, 80% of them were against the vision? A year's hard work produces 4% in favor! What drawing board would you go back to with respect to next steps?

You could be a principal in one of Chicago's STARS (School Leadership Teams for Achieving Results for Students) schools, in which you and four or five teachers form a school leadership team and participate in a series of six to eight annual professional development sessions along with teams from 25 or so other schools. How do you use this opportunity to develop your own school? What skills do you need to learn from other schools in the cohort and to contribute to their learning within the network? And should you have any worries now that your high-profile superintendent, Arne Duncan, has departed to become Obama's secretary of education?

What would be your change strategy if, in 2000, you were the newly appointed dean of education of the University of Pretoria, South Africa, expected to change 100 years of tradition in an all-white university? As the first black person—let alone being the dean of the place—Jonathan Jansen found himself in this position as he arrived at the parking lot gate his first day on the job and said, "Good evening, comrades. I am the new dean of education; can I get my keys?" The two white gate attendants doubled over in laughter. "Yeah, right," said one of them. "And I'm Bishop Tutu." Luckily Jonathan knew something about the skinny of tough change, and proceeded to change the culture of the faculty over the next seven years. We will catch up to him in Chapter 8 to get an idea of how he handled trust, resistance, and love to make profound changes in a remarkably short time.

What skills do you need to learn from other schools in the cohort and to contribute to their learning within the network?

Tim Brighouse was the CEO of Birmingham's local education authority, running well over 500 schools in a deprived multiethnic urban setting. He went on to become the czar of the London Challenge that attempted to change the quality and reputation of what it means to be a teacher in greater London—a workforce of over 60,000 teachers and school heads. What would you do with the advice he gives to young leaders? First he advises, if you are being questioned by your superiors or the media about a particular matter and you don't know the answer, for heaven's sake don't "blag" and fake the answer. Don't be afraid to say you don't know, but you will find out and report back. (He does say that you should know enough so that you don't have to say this every time.) Second, he says if you are in charge and something goes wrong because of the mistake of a subordinate, take the blame, accept the responsibility, and don't leave your people out to dry. Would following this advice make you more change savvy?

What about Finland? Coming from nowhere 30 years ago, the Finnish educational system ranks first these days in literacy, math, and science among over 40 OECD (Organisation for Economic Co-operation and Development) countries in the carefully conducted Program for International Student Assessments (PISA) of student learning. This has prompted waves of visits by educators around the world seeking to find the secret to Finland's success. You ask the minister of education for an explanation as to how they did it, and he responds, "I don't know, we really don't have a strategy." We do know

Tim Brighouse, England's "Change Czar"

Source: Tim Brighouse, http://www.50lessons.com/viewlesson.asp?l=1010

that the teachers have high status and qualifications (every teacher is required to have a master's degree). But how helpful is it to know that, especially when the minister can't explain how they did it? And if he can't explain the strategy, how likely is Finland to remain on top?

These 13 change problems from five different countries, all ones that we know or have been associated with, seem as different as chalk and cheese, but they are all about motion leadership. This is the knowledge and skill base we have been working on. We are not interested in success stories in this or that school or even a string of unconnected schools. Our work is about *whole-system reform.* Change-savvy knowledge concerns what leaders need to know and are able to do with all schools in the district, province or state, or country (see Fullan, 2010).

We are not interested in success stories in this or that school or even a string of unconnected schools. Our work is about *whole-system reform.*

Motion leadership is different because it gets inside movement. There is little benefit in describing already successful cases if you don't know how they got that way. We want to get inside the process and read between the lines to get a real sense of the action. So think movement, positive motion, and new and improved direction. Think how does one change the status quo and overcome inertia—inertia, after all, is not lack of movement (things like to do what they are already doing). We are thus talking about changing direction for the better—dynamic, exciting, the boiled-down essence of how to make the complex simpler and more powerful.

Think movement, positive motion, and new and improved direction.

Why talk about the skinny on change? When it comes to change, less is more. A few great insights can yield heaps of good motion much more so than the most sophisticated strategic plan. The skinny gets at the smallest number of powerful things you should know about getting motion. We get at this with as much crystal clarity as possible. This will not make you instantly change savvy—no one ever became savvy by being spoon-fed. But it will set you on the right path armed with enough insight to accelerate what you are able to accomplish.

The skinny is about reducing the weight of the change train. There is too much overload and baggage on the current change journey. The skinny is about "simplexity"—finding the smallest number of high-leverage, easy-to-understand actions that unleash stunningly powerful consequences. This is what Oliver Wendell Holmes was getting at when he said, "I wouldn't give a fig for simplicity on this side of complexity but I would give my life for simplicity on the other side of complexity." The skinny is the best ideas on the other side of complexity. It strips away overloaded change—cluttered commotion—and gives us the essential core of what we need in order to get real change owned by the critical mass. It is what Matthew May (2009) talks about in his treatment of "elegance." Elegance is the subtraction of weight so that you end up with the essence of the issue. The skinny of change is the search and use of ideas that have maximum impact with concise effort. There is an old Irish expression, "Never trust a skinny chef." Let's do trust a skinny change agent; but skinny is not scrawny. Skinny change agents punch way above their weight. Let's see what it takes to become a skinny change agent.

The skinny is about "simplexity"—finding the smallest number of high-leverage, easy-to-understand actions that unleash stunningly powerful consequences.

CHAPTER THREE

CHANGE ITSELF

In 1982, Peters and Waterman offered the metaphor "ready-fire-aim" to capture the action bias of high-performing companies that they studied. The concept was intuitively appealing but it was hard to find the savvy in there. It turns out that they were right, and we now have good evidence of the particular operational meaning of that famous phrase—and rich in insights it truly is.

There is a tight cluster of change-savvy ideas embedded in "ready-fire-aim" wisdom, and we will discuss them in turn (see Figure 3.1).

Figure 3.1 Ready-Fire-Aim

- Relationships first (too fast/too slow)
- Honor the implementation dip
- Beware of fat plans
- Behaviors before beliefs
- Communication during implementation is paramount
- Learn about implementation during implementation
- Excitement prior to implementation is fragile
- Take risks and learn
- It is okay to be assertive

Figure 3.1 contains a lot of insights for one metaphor!

RELATIONSHIPS FIRST

Think about the last time you were appointed to a new leadership position and you were heading for your first day on the job. These days, all newly appointed leaders, by definition, have a mandate to bring about change. The first problem the newcomer faces is the too-fast-too-slow dilemma. If the leader comes on too strong, the culture will rebel (and guess who is leaving town—cultures don't leave town). If the leader is overly respectful of the existing culture, he or she will become absorbed into the status quo. What to do? Take in the following good advice from Herold and Fedor (2008). Change-savvy leadership, they say, involves

- careful entry to the new setting;
- listening to and learning from those who have been there longer;
- engaging in fact finding and joint problem solving;
- carefully (rather than rashly) diagnosing the situation;
- forthrightly addressing people's concerns;
- being enthusiastic, genuine, and sincere about the change circumstances;
- obtaining buy-in for what needs fixing; and
- developing a credible plan for making that fix.

What should strike you is not the charismatic brilliance of the new leaders but their "careful entry," "listening," and "engaging in fact finding and joint problem solving." In other words, attend to the new relationships that have to be developed. There are situations, of course, where the culture is so toxic the leader may need to clean house. Or there might be one "derailer" that stands out, whom few like, and who requires immediate action (get the wrong people off the bus), but by and large, leaders must develop relationships first to a degree before they can push challenges. You get only one chance to make a first impression, and it had better be a good one—not too fast, nor too slow.

Steve Munby, when he was appointed the CEO of the National College of School Leaders in England in 2001 (recently renamed National College for Leadership of Schools and Children's Services), knew about the too-fast-too-slow skinny. The National College had lost its focus under the previous CEO, trying to be all things to all people. Steve knew that refocusing was essential. He had some ideas, but the first thing he did was make 500 phone calls to school heads across the country asking them what the college meant to them, what it could do to serve them better, and so on. One month later (it takes a while to phone 500 people and make a personal connection), he had conveyed to the country that change was coming and that he was going to listen and act. The college went on to reestablish a strong presence in the field, helping to develop school leaders across the country and to prepare and support the next generation of school heads. He moved fast, but not too fast, and he was careful to build relationships as he went.

> If the leader comes on too strong, the culture will rebel.

I have already referred to Sallyann Stanton, who used this insight to get the right speed to involve a resistant teacher leader and in turn to get a whole group of teachers onboard. It is difficult to make yourself slow down in order to get greater acceleration later, especially if you have strong moral purpose, as all of our change-savvy leaders do.

This was a lesson that Greg Mortenson had to learn in working with local leaders in northern Pakistan and Afghanistan in building schools mostly for girls (Mortenson & Relin, 2009). In this remarkable change story, Greg, driven by moral purpose and a sense of desperate urgency (literally, children had no school building to go to), spent from sunrise to sunset at the construction site of his first school. Progress was too slow for his liking as he tried to cope with various delays as workers had other priorities to attend to. At one point, the local village leader, Haji Ali, took him aside and said, "You have done much for my people and we appreciate it. But now you must do one more thing for me" (p. 149). Greg replied he'd do anything. Here was Haji's request:

> Sit down. And shut your mouth. You're making everyone crazy. . . . If you want to thrive in Baltistan you have to respect our ways. The first time you share tea with a Balti, you are a stranger. The second time you take tea, you are an honored guest. The third time you share a cup of tea, you become family, and for our family, we are prepared to do anything, even die. . . . Dr. Greg, you must take time to share three cups of tea. (p. 150)

Says Greg, "That day, Haji Ali taught me the most important lesson I've ever learned in my life . . . to slow down and make building relationships as important as building projects" (p. 150).

Three weeks later, the building was finished and Greg Mortenson went on to help local villagers build 81 schools, including 15 in Afghanistan, all in slightly more than a decade—with 9/11 smack in the middle.

HONOR THE IMPLEMENTATION DIP

For a long time, we have had the finding that when you try something new, even if there has been some preimplementation preparation, the first few months are bumpy. How could it be otherwise? New skills and understandings require a learning curve. Once we brought this out in the open, a lot of people immediately felt better to know that it is normal and everyone goes through it. Second, this finding led to the realization that we needed to focus on capacity building at this critical stage. Along come Herold and Fedor, who find the same phenomenon in business. And they furnish additional insights (see Figure 3.2).

Figure 3.2 The Myth and the Reality of Change

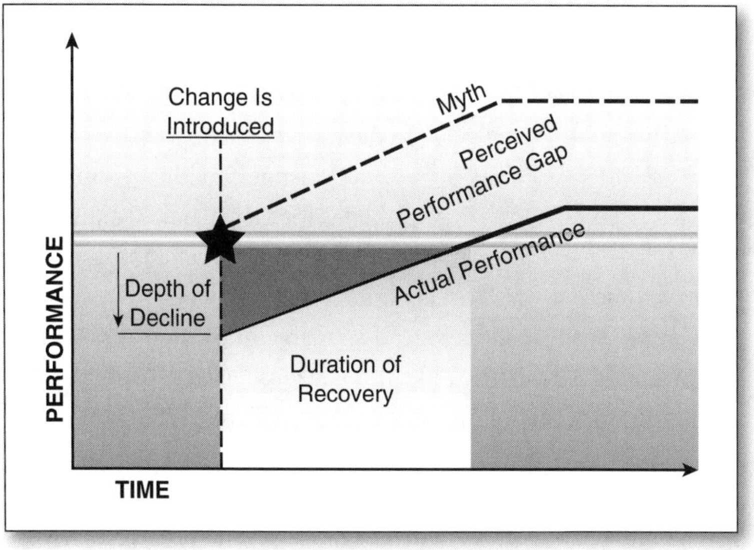

Source: Herold and Fedor, 2008.

Three things stand out. First is the myth of change. Those who introduce the change (usually far removed from the implementation scene) assume that there will be some immediate gains. It can't be thus—by definition. Second, look inside the "depth of decline" triangle. If you are an implementer, the costs to you are immediate and concrete, while the benefits are distant and theoretical. Thus the cost-benefit ratio is out of whack in favor of the negative.

Third, if you are a leader, here is the skinny: Don't expect many compliments! People are not having a good time. Leaders, therefore, have to be aware that their job is to help people get through the dip. In effect, change-savvy leadership works to increase the upward slope of the bottom line of the triangle (decreasing the duration of recovery) so that the breakthrough line to the plus side occurs sooner—within six months in our best efforts.

Our change-savvy leaders with deep moral purpose learn to overcome the inevitable first barriers. Jamie Oliver (2009), starting into what looked like a straightforward problem (get kids to eat good-tasting food that is infinitely better for them), quickly stumbled into the implementation dip. And he stayed there a while, lamenting more than once, "I have never banged my head against the wall so many times" and "God, I feel so uninspired. I can't work like this because I have to be inspired to work. I am so far out of my comfort zone with respect to what I normally cook. I am getting so grumpy. I am confused and harassed. These are the most humbling days I have ever had as a chef." Jamie had natural change savvy, and as we will see, he found other ways to move forward including how to meet the limits of the budget that called for a unit cost per meal of 37 pence (about 63 cents).

Leaders have to be aware that their job is to help people get through the dip.

Has Jamie hit the wall in trying to get kids to change their eating habits?

Our change leaders are parsimonious in using a small number of powerful forces that get breakthrough results—such as having immense moral commitment to a cause along with a clump of empathy with those they are dealing with. This combination of resolute leadership and empathy enables these leaders to find alternative ways when they get stuck. They demonstrate persistence with flexibility but never stray from the core purpose. Jamie has it.

> A combination of resolute leadership and empathy enables leaders to find alternative ways when they get stuck. They demonstrate persistence with flexibility but never stray from the core purpose.

BEWARE OF FAT PLANS

We have found that there is a natural tendency for leaders to over- plan "on paper." Our colleague Doug Reeves (2009) captures it wonderfully: "The size and the prettiness of the plan is inversely related to the quality of action and the impact on student learning" (p. 81). Once you say this, it becomes obvious. Why are planning and plans so seductive? There are *no people* on those pages! PowerPoint slides don't talk back.

> We have found that there is a natural tendency for leaders to overplan "on paper." Why are planning and plans so seductive? There are *no people* on those pages! PowerPoint slides don't talk back.

This does not mean you should skip the planning cycle. After all, there is "ready" in the ready-fire-aim trio. So do focus on the right priorities. Do attend to relationships. But get to action sooner, and treat it as a learning period. Go light on judgment at this stage. Mintzberg (2004) has it right when he observes that early planning-implementation is more like "strategizing" than it is like "strategy."

Once again, skinny prevails. Time and again, Reeves found that fat plans don't move. He offers instead the metaphor (indeed, offers a specific district example) of the "one-page plan" (2009, p. 83). In advocating making plans as simple as possible, but not more so, he concludes, "There is evidence that schools are well served by one-page plans that are clearly focused and sufficiently simple so that all participants in the process understand their role in executing the plans" (p. 83). Less is more if you know the essence of motion leadership. For example, York Region District, a large multicultural district just north of Toronto, had a 45-page improvement plan in 2007, then a 22-page plan in 2008,

> Do not load up on vision, evidence, and sense of urgency. Rather, give people new experiences in relatively nonthreatening circumstances, and build on it.

and an 8-page plan in 2009. The more you know, the briefer you get. That's skinny talk.

BEHAVIOR BEFORE BELIEFS

Research on attitudinal change has long found that most of us change our behaviors somewhat before we get insights into new beliefs. The implication for approaching new change is clear. Do not load up on vision, evidence, and sense of urgency. Rather, give people new experiences in relatively nonthreatening circumstances, and build on it, especially through interaction with trusted peers (Chapter 4)—very simple but hard to do when you are impatient for buy-in.

Jamie Oliver started with one secondary school, named Kidbrooke. After being depressed by what the kids were eating (nutritionists and doctors at the local hospital reported huge numbers of cases of constipation in preteens, including finding unformed feces backing up into their stomachs), Jamie became even more determined to do something about it. His first challenge was Nora, the head dinner lady who would have no part of his fancy ways—she has over 1,000 mouths to feed, on time, and at 37 pence a stomach. He tried to work alongside Nora but couldn't do anything right according to her. Partly for his own sanity ("I have to get her out of the kitchen") and partly to have her experience firsthand what it is like to cook properly, he arranged for her to spend a week working with his chefs at his famous London restaurant, Fifteen. His head chef, Arthur Potts, began to teach Nora basic knife skills in cutting vegetables, then he moved on to not overcooking, then to a rule that Nora never heard of—never send a new dish out that you haven't tasted (she did taste one of Arthur's dishes, but it was so delicious she sat down and ate the whole bowl). Gradually, these new behaviors began to make sense to Nora, and she started to alter her beliefs (but not before a few dozen more change obstacles).

COMMUNICATION DURING IMPLEMENTATION IS PARAMOUNT

Put directly, communication during implementation is far more important than communication prior to implementation. Recall Wendy Thomson, who spent a year talking up the vision in all quarters of the organization only to discover that, at best, 4% favored the new direction. Why is this so? Communication in the abstract, in the absence of action, means almost nothing.

> Communication in the abstract, in the absence of action, means almost nothing.

Once you start action—"fire" in our language—communication means something concrete for better or worse. The change-savvy leader accomplishes several critical things at this stage. Problems get identified through constant two-way communication. Information is based on the specific happenings. Second, the leader has multiple opportunities to communicate and refine the vision in relation to concrete implementation and—this is crucial—to state the essence (i.e., the skinny) of the implementation strategy itself. In short, problems get solved, a we-we identity around a common vision gets strengthened, and people come to know the implementation strategy

Dalton McGuinty in Ontario exemplifies this principle. Despite being premier with a host of other demanding responsibilities, McGuinty always stays close to the action. Here, he is in a project called "Leader to Leader," in which he meets four times a year with a group of 20 school principals (10 from difficult schools that have had success, and 10 from schools that are still struggling). The discussion is focused on what it is like to be a leader in tough times; what he faces, for example, in the financial recession with its crushing priorities, what the school principals are dealing with, what's working, and what are the most difficult problems at hand. He creates and responds to every opportunity he can because as he said in a recent speech to a group of state leaders in Washington, D.C., the first lesson is that "the drive to make progress cannot be a fad." You have to stay the course on the ground. McGuinty's second lesson is that "education is not important to the government if it is not important to the head of the government" (McGuinty, 2009). He knows that you have to communicate and listen every day during implementation.

Premier Dalton McGuinty initiated the "Leader to Leader" program, a principal-mentoring group he works with in Ontario.

© Todd Korol/Reuters/Corbis

LEARN ABOUT IMPLEMENTATION DURING IMPLEMENTATION

One of the most powerful strategies we have employed is to find different ways for implementers to learn from other implementers, especially those in similar circumstances who are further down the line. I referred earlier to Ontario's Schools on the Move strategy where 150 schools that have had three successive years of improvement in literacy and numeracy are identified, examined as to how they did it, and then given resources to help other schools in similar circumstances. This is not a "why can't you be more like your brother" strategy but rather a recognition that this is very

> Find different ways for implementers to learn from other implementers, especially those in similar circumstances who are further down the line.

hard work, some are figuring it out, and we can learn from them. Effective leaders realize that many of the answers are out there, in pockets, and that one rich strategy is to draw on and spread the wisdom of the crowds. I take this up in more detail in Chapter 4 with examples from Tower Hamlets and Ontario.

EXCITEMENT PRIOR TO IMPLEMENTATION IS FRAGILE

If your anticipation is greater than your fulfillment, then you are not very good at implementation. Excitement in advance of doing something is understandable, but it does not have much of a foundation. Indeed, the fall in the implementation dip will be even greater if high aspirations precede it. Premature excitement is no substitute for the hard work of implementation (they don't call it *fire* for nothing). Everything we know about motivation tells us that deep excitement comes from doing something worthwhile, doing it well, and getting results. You can get none of this during planning or vision sessions. You have to earn and experience excitement; you can't fake it.

Thus, knowledgeable change leaders strive for small early successes, acknowledge real problems, admit mistakes, protect their people as Tim Brighouse did, and celebrate success along the way. They avoid phony pep rallies. They love genuine results that generate great pride in the organization. They have their finger on

> Everything we know about motivation tells us that deep excitement comes from doing something worthwhile, doing it well, and getting results.

the energy pulse of people, knowing that it will ebb and flow but will be spurred by positive results.

Excitement during implementation when it occurs is solidly based on substance. York Region, for example, holds an annual learning fair in which every one of its 190 schools prepares a 25-minute, multimedia presentation. They present what they set out to accomplish at the beginning of the year, what measurable results they obtained, strategies used, obstacles encountered, lessons learned, and so on. Talk about excitement! The room is abuzz with emotion. As one participant says, "It is days like this that I wish were 36 hours long." People cannot get enough. It is real and spontaneous because it is about what is actually being done. If you ask participants to describe the learning fair in one word, the most frequent utterance is "energizing."

TAKE RISKS AND LEARN

Jamie McCracken was a high school vice principal and principal in Ottawa Catholic District School Board for six years and served in the district office for a few years before he was appointed director, or superintendent, of the district. He knew the culture of the district from the inside and uses a wonderful skinny word to describe it: *clenched.* Everything was tight; people were afraid to act, so they played it safe and kept to themselves. The district also had no consistent focus announcing a dozen or so "thrusts" each year (definitely not a skinny word) that changed year after year; no matter, because the thrusts were easily ignored.

As soon as he became director, Jamie set out to change the culture. He consulted widely and announced three priorities—success for students, success for staff, and stewardship of resources. These priorities have remained the same for the past seven years. To pursue the goals, Jamie made it clear that people should try new things and learn from their experiences. Risk taking as learning became the district's modus operandi. The district framed the reform around some of the most powerful "all systems go" strategies we know (see Fullan, 2010, for the particulars about the Ottawa story), but the main point is that there was a license to innovate and problem solve. Today, Ottawa is the highest performing large district in Ontario in literacy and numeracy, having moved steadily some 10 or more percentage points in reading, writing, and math, and in high school graduation in the past four years across all of its 84 schools. People are engaged, energized, and collectively committed to continuous improvement. The skinny on risk taking is known by all organizations that are consistently successful, such as Toyota, whose leaders embrace the philosophy of "we view errors as opportunities for learning" (Liker & Hoseus, 2008, p. 40). Ready, fire, aim represents purposeful learning and taking learning risks is embedded in the psyche of successful organizations.

IT'S OKAY TO BE ASSERTIVE

Many of the potentially best leaders in these democratic times are often reticent to assert themselves. To know about change is to know about inertia, which is to say that sometimes the status quo needs a wakeup call. You can't wait for success, you have to kick-start it. Leadership is a mixture of authority and democracy. Leaders can get away with being assertive under three

> You can't wait for success, you have to kick-start it.

conditions: (1) when they have built trusted relationships, (2) when it turns out they have a good idea, and (3) when they empower people from day one to help assess and shape the idea.

Do you think Jamie Oliver was holding back when he said, "This food is crap. I wouldn't serve it to my dog"? Did Dalton McGuinty conduct a series of consultative meetings when he was elected in 2003 on whether literacy, numeracy, and high school graduation rates would be his government's core priorities? No, these leaders just went ahead and acted using their change savvy to empower people and problem solve as they went. Remember, being assertive is only one part of being change savvy. These leaders do not go around making random assertions. They learn first and always as they go. They are relentless—another of Dalton's lessons: "If you want to achieve your goals, you have to keep up the pressure—all the time" (McGuinty, 2009).

In essence, change-savvy leaders know a great deal because they are learners (along the lines of the knowledge in this book). As such, they do come to know a lot, and to be quick in sizing up complex situations. They are more likely to get their responses right. But they also respect complexity and live by the definition of wisdom cited earlier—wisdom is using your knowledge while doubting what you know (Pfeffer & Sutton, 2008). In brief, if you want to get anything done, you have to combine assertiveness and humility.

The point of this treatment of considering the nine elements of "change itself" has been to bring operational meaning to the ready-fire-aim metaphor. These elements

If you want to get anything done, you have to combine assertiveness and humility.

synergize into a bias for purposeful action. The skinny goes like this:

- To get anywhere, you have to *do* something.
- In doing something, you need to focus on developing *skills.*
- Acquisition of skills increases *clarity.*
- Clarity results in *ownership.*
- Doing this together with others generates *shared ownership.*
- Persist no matter what. *Resilience* is your best friend.

Motion leadership with these ingredients produces seemingly magical results and paradoxically can be accomplished by any group that pays attention to and masters the skinny of change. Let's take Rideau Elementary School in Limestone District School Board—the school that Ben Levin (2008) visited when he was deputy minister of education in Ontario. Here was a school with "ordinary" teachers that had 300 or so high-need students. When they started three years ago to seriously address the situation, the school had fewer than 20% of its students reaching the province's standard in sixth-grade reading. At the beginning, few teachers believed that their particular school was capable of improvement. They also felt that with a large number of behavioral issues, students' personal problems needed to be addressed before things like reading could be taught. Fast-forward three years, and you find that 70% of the school's sixth-grade students are meeting the high provincial standard. The teachers, says Ben, are "fiercely proud" of what they have achieved (Levin, 2008, p. 108). What happened?

Basically, with focused leadership internal and external to the school, they zeroed in on effective instructional reading practices.

With the help of an external literacy coach and the direct involvement of the principal, the teachers learned new teaching practices together.

What seemed impossible at the beginning was not all that hard in retrospect.

Three years later, "they owned these practices" (Levin, 2008, p. 108). The teachers said they would never go back to their old ways, and they realized that "any school could do something similar" (p. 108). What seemed impossible at the beginning was not all that hard in retrospect. It was difficult, but it was accompanied by new skill acquisition, a sense of camaraderie, and an increasingly energizing force of motion in action feeding on itself. Problems were encountered, but they were in the context of getting somewhere. Motion leadership takes the mystery out of complexity and accelerates positive change. Ready-fire-aim—three words—is a skinny metaphor that packs a nine-gauge punch (as in Figure 3.1).

Motion leadership takes the mystery out of complexity.

Now you see why ready-fire-aim is the correct sequence. Focused meaning comes out the other end. None of this is mechanical. It requires touch. Leaders must learn to become change savvy by reflective doing. It's messy at first, but you eventually get somewhere, and get good at doing it. It works because the group develops capacity and begins to believe in themselves because they see the results. You and the group become more at ease with difficult problems. You go skinny, as in focusing on the smallest number of things that you can describe clearly

Leaders must learn to become change savvy by reflective doing.... It works because the group develops capacity and begins to believe in themselves because they see the results.

to others and that have amazing simplexity power. You reassure others as you help them develop. All in all, you as leader and the group you are working with start to understand change itself. You have a big leg up on others. You are ready for more action.

Focus: Frosh outlook
All grades writing
Math

One-page plan

CHAPTER FOUR

CONNECT PEERS WITH PURPOSE

The skinny, as I have said, is to get to the essence of the matter. There are reams of articles and books written about collaboration, professional learning communities, and the like. Now it is time to seek the concise meaning of getting peers to interact on a focused basis. To meet our criteria, the insights here must be both skinny and powerful.

It may seem odd to ask the question, why collaborate? but it is essential for leaders to understand its deeper meaning. The problem that purposeful collaboration solves is how to get focus and coherence in otherwise fragmented systems. Top-down change doesn't work—people resist when leaders try to tighten things up. The track record for bottom-up change (let a thousand flowers bloom) is not any better. If left on their own, some people will flourish, while others languish.

> Top-down change doesn't work—people resist when leaders try to tighten things up. . . . The best way to tighten things up is to get peers to do it.

It turns out that the best way to tighten things up is to get peers to do it. Thus, the role of the leader is to enable, facilitate, and cause peers to interact in a focused manner. Peer interaction is the *social glue* of focus and cohesion (see Fullan, 2008).

I have just given you a piece of theory. As with other aspects of motion leadership, this theoretical clarity derives from practice. And as with all of these matters, by studying and facilitating motion, we learn the particulars. Let's take four examples: intraschool, interschool or clusters, whole systems, and then Tower Hamlets—how in the world did they get all 100 or so school leaders to pull together under the most difficult circumstances?

> The role of the leader is to enable, facilitate, and cause peers to interact in a focused manner. Peer interaction is the *social glue* of focus and cohesion.

Within-school (or *intraschool*) collaboration, when it is focused, produces powerful results on an ongoing basis. There is a great deal written about professional learning communities. No need to summarize it here except to say that the term travels a lot better than the concept. And while instructional leadership of principals is all the rage, it is not really clear what this looks like in practice. So let's examine the matter up close.

In terms of the link between a principal's action and student learning, there is one finding that stands out in time as more powerful than any other, and it is this: the degree to which the principal participates as a *learner* in helping teachers figure out how to get classroom and schoolwide improvement (Robinson, Lloyd, & Rowe, 2008). When Gord Wagner was principal of Jersey Public School in York Region, you can see him in one of our videos (York Region District School Board, 2007) sitting down with groups of teachers, examining student writing examples according to their quality vis-à-vis specific standards, jointly making the link to particular instructional practices tracking the progress of each and every student, and identifying changes in practice that would increase student learning. Jersey students doubled their proficiency in the demanding Ontario provincial assessments, from 32% to 63%—a high achievement in three years. Gord was a lead learner, causing motion through peers.

What is happening in Jersey and with other principals who learn how to connect peers with purpose is that they participate directly. They don't dominate—they respect the expertise of teachers—but they are experts in moving the group along. They push for precision and specificity; they link instruction to practice. They foster transparency of outcomes and practice.

Several key things are accomplished simultaneously within this one strategy—good practice flows, poor practice diminishes, and a shared sense of purpose and commitment gets generated. As a result of participating in this process, the individual teacher does not think of just the children in his or her classroom but becomes committed to *our* children, in the school as a whole. We call this the *we-we commitment,* and it is powerful.

The individual teacher does not think of just the children in his or her classroom but becomes committed to *our* children, in the school as a whole. We call this the *we-we commitment,* and it is powerful.

If school leaders stop there (i.e., think that strong intraschool collaboration is it), they are doomed to go the way of the dodo bird. Schools as islands mean that they are cut off from other sources of support and pressure. That is why we have come to the conclusion that each and every school *must* become part of a network or cluster, again with focus and specificity. The Chicago schools in the STARS program and York Region schools in their

Learning Networks (each involving 6 to 10 schools) and in their annual learning fair are doing exactly what Gord Wagner is doing, only on a larger scale. They are purposeful, they are specific, they learn to link practice with outcomes. They learn and share and learn. Their shared moral commitment goes sky high.

Being in a purposeful network gives you more support and more "positive pressure" to improve. If you have to explain yourself to other schools, as in the Chicago and York Region cases, you get sharper. If you see what other schools are doing, you get stimulated. Time and again we observe the value of "friendly competition" as schools try to outdo each other. Negative competition dissolves. Pride in the net product increases. The we-we commitment strikes again.

Time and again we observe the value of "friendly competition" as schools try to outdo each other. Negative competition dissolves. Pride in the net product increases.

At a third level (beyond clusters) of schools—whole large districts, or whole states or provinces—the same strategy can be, indeed must be, employed if you are going to get whole-system reform. We are doing this in the province of Ontario. The literacy and numeracy secretariat directly and indirectly deliberately employs the principles of purposeful peer interaction. The Student Success strategy uses the skinny change principles to stimulate mutual learning in the 900 high schools in Ontario. Local change agents, innovative programming, personalizing learning, and explicit monitoring combine to engage students, thereby increasing their own learning. As a result, there is a steady 2% gain in high school graduation results for five straight years, increasing the retention rates from 68% to 77% over the period (plenty of examples of what system movement looks like are provided in *All Systems Go* [Fullan, 2010]).

The Schools on the Move strategy, mentioned earlier, has identified 150 schools in the province that are making extraordinary progress in improving literacy and numeracy achievement for their students. These schools are identified by name, profiled, and given resources to help other interested schools learn from them. The whole atmosphere is that this is very hard and complex work; some people are figuring out how to do it. The strategy makes it easy to learn from peers who are having success.

Tower Hamlets is a very interesting case. One of the most deprived areas in all of England, over an 11-year period, 1996–2007, they outperformed the country in terms of growth on every measure of student achievement. At the beginning, their literacy proficiency score (for 11-year-olds) was 35% (compared to the national average of 58%). By 2007, Tower Hamlets equaled the national average of 80%. Same for math, same for science, ditto for secondary school results—they performed way above expectations. How did they do it?

> Once school leaders see the slightly bigger picture and get to know each other in a common endeavor of great moral purpose, they thrive on "competitive collaboration."

In working on peer learning across schools over the past decade, we often hear at the outset that schools won't cooperate because they are competing for the same pupils, or they are only interested in their own fate, and we've even heard the notion that if other schools do poorly, better-performing schools look better by comparison. Once we got into it—the doing of cross-school learning—the issue of competition dissolved in virtually every case. We wondered about the dynamic.

Tower Hamlets provides the answer. Alan Boyle (2009) studied Tower Hamlets as part of a larger project called "Beyond

Expectations," led by Andy Hargreaves and Alma Harris. Alan found that once school leaders saw the bigger picture and got to know each other in a common endeavor of great moral purpose, they thrived on "competitive collaboration." They enjoy trying to outdo each other for the common good even to the point of sharing ideas in a catch-me-if-you-can spirit. But it takes careful change savvy by district and school leaders. Alan Boyle (2009) captures it well with reference to four powerful factors. Here is the skinny on competitive collaboration.

First, notes Alan, there needs to be "resolute leadership" at the top (Jamie and Dalton, take a bow). In Tower Hamlets, with successive CEOs there has been a culture of high expectations where no excuses are acceptable, with a shared focus for action. "It *moves,*" says Alan, "from intention, through specific actions to achievement by setting ambitious targets, refusing to be deflected from the core priorities and purposely combining short-term gains in test scores with long-term development of the whole child" (p. 13, italics added).

> Collective responsibility is associated with moral purpose.

Second, and this is at the heart of this chapter, they experienced and built on the power of "allegiance" to each other, fed by both central leadership and some key school heads over a five-year period. Collective responsibility is associated with moral purpose. School and district leaders, I am going to say, *discovered* the value of solidarity. As experiences of mutual help accumulated, people began to trust each other in a common cause. *Allegiance,* according to Alan, reflects and "demonstrates a genuine collective responsibility with full commitment to the cause" (p. 18). And, "there is positive competition between them to achieve the highest results across a fairly level playing field" (p. 19). The outcomes of such competitive loyalty are cohesion among the schools and stability in terms of continuous improvement. There is a palpable competitive edge between the schools. The unspoken message is that

> if they can do it why can't we. . . . It is not the kind of competiveness that leads to boasting about your school's accomplishments. It is more about competing with yourself to be as good as anyone else. (p. 25)

> The skinny is that nothing succeeds like collective capacity.

Third and fourth, Alan found that "professional power" was unleashed, and conditions for "sustainability" became more and more established. These two forces are clearly simplexity phenomena. Arising from resolute leadership and peer and hierarchical allegiance, professional power generates and focuses all possible resources on the problems to be addressed: "This attribute involves gathering all available resources and using them purposefully to gain most impact" (p. 21). In the process, sustainability gets built in—leaders developing future leaders who will carry on. The whole system becomes devoted to innovation and risk taking to improve the quality of teaching and learning, supporting leadership development, cultivating peer learning within and across schools, and supporting schools in trouble.

A test of Tower Hamlets solidarity occurred in 2007 when they rejected government pressure to set up a City Academy (a single, highly resourced lead school). Even though it meant refusing a

> You need to learn about implementation during implementation.

potload of money, their change savvy told them that this would be a divisive move. Once you have change savvy, it saves a lot of time and grief. It took the secondary head teachers slightly more than a nanosecond to unanimously oppose the City Academy because they knew it would threaten cohesion, collaboration, and—paradoxically—innovation in the district as a whole, innovation essential for continuous improvement for the benefit of all.

All four of the above examples follow the same principle. You need to learn about implementation during implementation. You need to do it systematically so that it adds up. Good practice flows, poor practice declines, and people's sense of identity gets enlarged as they become committed to the larger enterprise. You need to develop solidarity and collaborative competition with respect to a bigger cause. The work becomes more elegantly effective. We see, in a word, the dynamic power of motion leadership.

Purposeful peer interaction works not because people fall in love with their hierarchical leaders but rather because positive peer bonds become ever strengthened. The skinny is that nothing succeeds like collective capacity. System reform will never be a success if only leaders are working on it. There are not enough leaders to go around. But there are enough peers. Al West, the CEO of SEI investments, put it best:

> Because we do all of our work in teams, working together is more important than managing up . . . The problem with hierarchies is that they require you to engineer everything in advance. (quoted in Taylor & LaBarre, 2006, pp. 239–240)

In short, being change savvy includes harnessing the power of peers, and both central and school leaders need to partner to do this. (For additional specific, precise, proof-positive evidence that purposeful peer interaction works to produce quality change in student engagement and achievement, see Dufour, Dufour, Eaker, & Karhanek, 2010.)

> System reform will never be a success if only leaders are working on it. There are not enough leaders to go around. But there are enough peers.

But still only a minority of systems employ the power of collective capacity (Fullan, 2010). If only we could get the vast majority of peers engaged. For that, we need what we have learned so far but also a few more elements of locomotion—such as capacity building with bite, but not with judgmentalism—another simple, elegant solution to a complex problem.

CHAPTER FIVE

CAPACITY BUILDING TRUMPS JUDGMENTALISM

If a leader notices something that needs improvement, he or she can either act on it or hope it will take care of itself. Acting on it constructively requires savvy. There are two powerful concepts involved: *capacity building* and *judgmentalism.* The skinny is to overuse the former and underuse the latter.

Capacity building concerns the knowledge, skills, and disposition of people individually but especially collectively. It is the group with shared purpose and skills that gets things done. You increase capacity in two ways, and leaders need to use both.

> Capacity building concerns the knowledge, skills, and disposition of people individually but especially collectively.

One way is to hire people with the appropriate capacities and potential in the first place. This includes making changes in key leadership positions sooner rather than later (get the right people on the bus). Mike McCue of Tellme Network gets it right when he says, "We look for people who light up when they are around other talented people" (in Taylor & LaBarre, 2006, p. 203). Hiring this way gives their organization a head start on capacity building.

Once people are on the job, continuous learning equals continuous capacity building. This is expressly the job of powerful peer learning (the previous chapter), and learning is the work (the next chapter). But there is one skill that is crucial and is particularly difficult to master and that is how to focus directly on things that need improvement without letting judgmentalism get in the way.

Judgmentalism is an odd term, not even in the dictionary, but it means perceiving something that is not working and wittingly or unwittingly conveying a negative or pejorative message. In our training, we typically ask small groups to discuss the following question: Is it possible to perceive something as ineffective and not be judgmental about it? I ask groups to answer the question yes or no and to provide their reason for so concluding. A long debate ensues that boils down to this: If you are an English teacher, the answer is, "No, it is not possible. To label something as ineffective is to make a judgment. Look it up in the dictionary." If you are a psychologist or change agent, the answer is yes. It is all in how you convey the issue of ineffectiveness. If it comes without attitude—"yes, this is ineffective, because it is hard, and we need to build capacity to deal with it"—there is a strong chance that movement will occur. To be nonjudgmental is to take the "ism" out of the equation.

Judgmentalism means perceiving something that is not working and wittingly or unwittingly conveying a negative or pejorative message.

Why is this important? Because change is about "moving" people. Moving is about motivating them to take new action. Savvy change leaders become good at identifying problems, being candid about their presence, and yet being empathetic enough that the person affected does not feel personally judged. Indeed, the best leaders make people feel good about working on and making progress relative to a tough problem or set of circumstances.

The best leaders make people feel good about working on and making progress relative to a tough problem or set of circumstances.

Let's return to Jamie's journey. With the utmost effort, and eventually with head dinner lady Nora's conversion to the cause, he became successful in Kidbrooke. He literally increased the skill (capacity) of the team of dinner ladies at the school to serve good, tasty, nutritious food within budget. Now, he said what we have accomplished won't be

Jamie Oliver prepares lunch for schoolchildren while head dinner lady Nora has a playful break.

instructive to others unless we can demonstrate that it can be done with a whole borough—in this case Greenwich with its 60 schools. To do this, Jamie had to combine capacity building with nonjudgmentalism.

He started by seeing what kids were eating, and he once again was shocked: "I honestly have no idea what is in this. I have never seen anything like this before. These kids are innocent, pure, their bodies and bones are going through the most important period of their lives. It is not right" (2009). He found one boy eating a tomato sauce sandwich. He discovered a mainstay of their diet: fried turkey twisters (which, upon analysis, contain only 30% turkey). He showed a group of children rhubarb, asparagus, and leeks, and very few could guess what they are. He asked another group what they like to eat, and they said chips and gravy, chips, twisters, and chocolate. He asked the boy who said chocolate what his second and third favorites are, and the boy replied, "Chocolate and chocolate." After a while, Jamie said, "I can't believe it. I think I am going to pass out."

Before tackling the big problem of 60 schools, he tried another small experiment with younger children in another borough, Durham, "the most unhealthy region in all of England." He took over a class and found none of them wanted any part of his diet, including Liam, who ate only pasta and rice. He finally got six class members who were willing to try his food and asked the others to leave. One little girl cried at being excluded, and Jamie allowed her back in to observe. The six "risk takers" enjoyed the new food, and Jamie built on it by having a food theme week, where songs about food are sung in every class, and people dress up as vegetables, including Jamie, who came as a cob of corn. More kids tucked into the delicious food, including Liam, whose parents reinforced his new eating habits. They noticed that Liam, who had previously been hyperactive all the time at home, became calm and relaxed. He faltered on the new diet and became hyper again—a half-hour after eating it; and later calmed again within 30 minutes of eating the better food. The parents—and even Jamie—were dumbfounded at the quickness of the impact. With his moral purpose buoyed, Jamie returned to Greenwich to tackle the whole borough and its 60 schools.

By this time, Jamie was becoming more change savvy, and he realized that he needed to get all 60 head dinner ladies onboard. He got one dinner lady, Leslie, to agree to try a new recipe that he provided with simple and clear directions. "I wanted to see what would happen," Jamie explained, "if I supplied only the recipe so that when I do the training, I will know what needs to be done." He visited Leslie on the job, and she told him, "I am having a nightmare doing this." She left out a key ingredient in the chicken recipe, saying, "Who wants lemon on chicken anyway?" Shocked by Leslie's cooking, Jamie realized that he was going to have to rethink the training, rewrite his recipes, and provide more support during implementation.

Having concluded that the key is to train all 60 head dinner ladies, he wisely recruited Nora (one of their peers, of course) from the pilot school, Kidbrooke, to help him. He tells Nora, "Unfortunately, the truth is that you have made yourself indispensible because you have done it." In a funny but tough capacity-building launch, he recruited the help of the military and their chefs to conduct a three-day boot camp on developing the capacity of the 60 school cooks (after all, the military must cook for masses and strive for nutritious food on a limited budget). The women were taught how to cut and prepare food and were given simple sample recipes that they had to follow under supervision. It was frustrating for all—"They just boil the buggery out of peas and broccoli," Jamie complained. And, "The butternut squash is totally wrong. There seems to be a hell of a lot of oil in there, girls," he told them. As an aside he uttered, "And they don't even taste what they make."

The ladies are not too happy either. Some of them rebel. "I can't do this. I can't keep up. This is not my life; it is just my job. It is slave labor. I don't think I can do this Monday to Friday; it is going to kill me. My legs are hurting. My arms are aching. It is too much." On day two, Jamie gave them a break and cooked dinner for them. The next day, the ladies tested their recipes on a whole brigade of 400 soldiers. Jamie told them, "If you overcook the broccoli, throw it out and do it again." In assessing the meal, he was encouraged—"7 out of 10," he said.

New capacities cannot be developed in three days, but it is a good start. Jamie explained to the dinner ladies that Nora was no different than any of them apart from the fact that she was six months further along. So he committed to troubleshooting and support for the dinner ladies as they returned to their schools. We will pick up this aspect of capacity building in the next chapter (learning is the work), but what about judgmentalism?

Jamie knew that the dinner ladies and their staff were terrible cooks. Amazingly, given his expertise and his urgent sense of moral purpose, he was not overly judgmental or negative. He has the empathy to recognize that these women are not really cooks. As he observed, "All they have ever done is reheat food that is delivered to the school. They don't cook. They reheat!" The change-savvy point is that Jamie combines capacity building and nonjudgmentalism. He could not make progress if he did not get this combination right—all under pressure-packed circumstances.

In education, Elizabeth City, Richard Elmore, and their colleagues (2009) at Harvard have captured the skinny of nonjudgmentalism in their work on *instructional rounds* (analogous to doctors' rounds). In making rounds of observations, they teach people the following principle: "description before analysis, analysis before prediction, prediction before evaluation" (p. 34). They have found that the hardest part of doing this work is to prevent people from jumping to early conclusions. Most people find it hard to be only descriptive as the starting point.

In our training, we ask people to identify a situation in which they received feedback, and to discuss whether they felt belittled or not at the time. In any large group, you get many examples of each. Then, we ask the people affected to attach a word that would capture their feelings. Those who felt judged come up with words like *frustrated, discouraged, incompetent,* and *alienated.* Those who did not feel belittled talk about being motivated and spurred to take action. As we say to leaders, the worst thing that you can do early in a relationship when you see something that you think should be changed is to roll your eyes (or the equivalent of such). This has nothing to do with whether you are right or wrong and only to do with whether you are going to get positive movement.

The worst thing that you can do early in a relationship when you see something that you think should be changed is to roll your eyes (or the equivalent of such). This has nothing to do with whether you are right or wrong and only to do with whether you are going to get positive movement.

Leaders who want to become savvier about change have to practice being nonjudgmental because it does not come naturally. This is hard to do, especially if you have a strong sense of moral purpose and urgency. As we saw in Jamie, it is possible to know that something is terribly ineffective and still have empathy and respect for people who have not had the opportunity to develop the capacity to become effective.

Judgment is a dish best served through the natural process of purposeful peer interaction, capacity building, and daily work—focus and use of transparent data.

This does not contradict my earlier point that in some toxic situations, you may have to remove certain people early. But by and large, if you want to get movement with a critical mass of people, you can't go around judging them. Judgment is a dish best served through the natural process of purposeful peer interaction, capacity building, and daily work—focus and use of transparent data.

Paradoxically, the more you park your judgment, and the more you play up capacity building, the more actual improvement you will get and the more that real accountability gets embedded. You literally create internal accountability where individuals and the group feel and take responsibility for their own progress. They are self-compelled to take corrective action when called for. This is not theory. It is what you see every time change-savvy leadership uses direct, nonjudgmental data along with capacity building. These leaders build individual and shared responsiblity in order to put external accountability in perspective (what I call, in *All Systems Go* [Fullan, 2010], "intelligent accountability").

Thus, add capacity building without negative judgment to your repertoire. Simplexity, once again—a single insight on the other side of complexity that generates powerful, albeit not always smooth, consequences. But still, you have launched capacity building only at the front end. For it to take hold, to go from 7 out of 10 to 9 or 10 out of 10, you have to do something that is even harder—make learning (i.e., make capacity building) the work that you do day after day. You and those you work with get better and better because you are learning how to do it in the setting in which you work. This is real change.

CHAPTER SIX

LEARNING IS THE WORK

When Peter Cole (2004) wrote an article with the intriguing title of "Professional Development: A Great Way to Avoid Change," what did he mean? He meant that what really counts is what happens *in between workshops*. Professional development sessions, walk-throughs, and site visits to other organizations can be valuable input, but you can't get "depth by visitation."

> There is only one way to get depth and that is at home through learning in the setting in which you work.

This is the hardest leadership challenge of them all—how do you build in learning for improvement day after day in your own organization? (See also Fullan, 2008.) Liker and Meier (2007), in their in-depth study of Toyota's culture, conclude that the biggest difference between Toyota and other organizations is *the depth of understanding* among Toyota employees regarding their work. We should say depth of *shared* understanding. There is only one way to get depth and that is in the daily workplace through learning in the setting in which you work.

When Gittell (2003) compared Southwest Airlines with all other airlines, she found that Southwest employees displayed "relational coordination" every day (as measured by shared goals, shared knowledge, mutual respect, frequent and timely communication, and problem-solving communication). Baggage handlers, flight attendants, ticket agents, cleanup crews, pilots, and other employees all behaved in this manner. How hard is it to keep this up in a tense, fast-paced enterprise like flying or teaching kids?

Malcolm Gladwell (2009) was talking about learning is the work when he described how successful "outliers" got that way by putting in "10,000 hours" of learning. He wrote a whole chapter on "The 10,000-hour rule." That sounds difficult enough, but motion leadership is harder, much harder, because Gladwell was referring to *individuals.* What about organizations such as York Region, which Lyn Sharratt and I wrote about in *Realization* (2009), with its 9,000 educators and 130,000 students? Let's try 100,000 hours of relational coordination—everybody being that good day after day.

A good example of learning is the work that can be seen in Armadale, the largest elementary school in York Region, with almost 900 students and 70 staff. Jill Maar, the principal, is a motion leader in action. She attends to all the core capacities that York has identified as essential for instructional success: examining the data and identifying trends, early and ongoing individualized intervention with those kids not doing so well, building the school leadership team, streamlining and focusing the budget, parent and family engagement, and being relentlessly attentive to the movement of the school. In one short year, 2008–2009, the school reduced the number of children at risk for each and every of the nine

> When motion leaders learn the skinny, they can greatly accelerate the pace of progress. Simplexity once again—a small number of things done well and in concert multiplies the effect and has built-in consequences of its own that literally get results fast and lay the foundation for even more.

grade levels from kindergarten to Grade 8—from 378 students to 233. Still a ways to go with one quarter of the students remaining at risk—but a far cry from the over 40% that the school started with: an amazing accomplishment in one year.

And their reading, writing, and math scores shot up some 15 percentage points in one year. Skinny change agents can move quickly because they focus on a small number of goals, use high-yield strategies, and are very specific in their actions. When motion leaders learn the skinny, they can greatly accelerate the pace of progress. Simplexity once again—a small number of things done well and in concert multiplies the effect and has built-in consequences of its own that literally get results fast and lay the foundation for even more. But fast successful change comes with its own risks. Can it really take hold that quickly? Is it solid or fragile? Does rapid success breed hubris in leaders? Skinny change agents stay thin by worrying about these kinds of questions.

Within learning is the work, such as at Armadale, people need to get better at two related things. First, they need to become more and more specific and precise in putting into place high-yield learning practices. As the best of these practices become evident, they need to come to have the status of being relatively nonnegotiable. We call this cluster of precision *consistency*. This is exactly what the 150 schools in Schools on the Move and the 190 York Region schools are doing. They are becoming more effective through relentless consistency and continuous improvement. When you see Gord Wagner, Jill Maar, and their teachers in York Region in action, they are focusing day after day on how well each and every student is doing, what the data tell them in particular, what changes in instruction are needed, and how much headway they are making. They go to training workshops held by York Region, but more than that, they apply the ideas in getting better and better at what they do. They become relentlessly consistent.

What about creativity and innovation? Does not relentless consistency crowd out the time for new ideas? Simplexity rears its head again. It is the people who are relentlessly consistent about achieving important goals who also seek continuous improvement. You can (and I am saying must) be both consistent and innovative. Change-savvy leaders who are relentlessly consistent are at the same time seeking continuous improvements.

You may have seen the 20 or so Tiger Woods ads put out by Accenture. Each ad shows Tiger in a different golf situation or depicting his fantastic swing and has a caption that adds up to 100%. One of these ads has the following observation: *Relentlessly consistent: 50%. Willingness to change: 50%.* These are Accenture's words, not mine.

Thus, the more committed you are to relentless consistency, the more naturally you seek improvements. Today's relentless consistency is tomorrow's innovation, and tomorrow's innovation is the next day's relentless consistency. At the beginning of a new change process, you need to become more consistent about the new way of doing things. Get better at what is known before branching out. This is capacity building, but it is in real time, on the job. And it is harder than preimplementation capacity building. Jamie Oliver (2009) found this out the hard way when he experienced that posttraining implementation was a nightmare compared to the initial three-day boot camp. But his empathy had already kicked in. The dinner ladies and me are going to be stretched, he noted: "They will be very frightened and worried." In actual implementation, the dinner ladies, still not good at the

The more committed you are to relentless consistency, the more naturally you seek improvements. Today's relentless consistency is tomorrow's innovation, and tomorrow's innovation is the next day's relentless consistency.

new cooking, went over budget, had to work overtime to complete everything, and found the pressure overwhelming. And the kids were still not taking to the new food with three-quarters of it ending up in the garbage bins. The canteen becomes a battleground. Jamie said, "I have nothing but fear for the dinner ladies, and I am definitely scared, out of my depth."

Even though postcamp implementation was phased in five schools each week, the problems piled up. Jamie and Nora kept providing on-the-scene support, a critical change-savvy action because it props up morale and builds further capacity with specific solutions and more skill development. But some of the dinner ladies were ready to give up, and Jamie, apparently knowing something about the implementation dip, said, "It is fucking day one, for crying out loud." He knew that he was trying them to the limit. He knew and told them that he realized they needed support. In week three, he borrowed some army chefs to help the dinner ladies. Note what is happening here: The work is harder because people are not yet good at it. As you develop capacity, the work gets easier, but they were not there yet.

Jamie and the crew were having a hard enough time with the first 15 schools, only 5,000 of the 20,000 kids he needed to affect. He expanded his strategy to include kids and their parents, including nine-year-old Luke, who refused to eat his food and when cajoled to eat some promptly threw it up on his plate in front of everyone. Jamie worked on strengthening the strategy before expanding to additional schools—better materials, involving the kids in cooking, having a food week in the school. It started to work. There was less wastage in the bins. They gave children stickers for doing a good job. Amazingly, Luke was happily eating the new food. The dinner ladies were still working harder than they did before, but they get satisfaction from the fact that they are cooking real food. They realize that they are actually becoming cooks, not "reheaters" of processed food prepared elsewhere.

Jamie noticed that even the trickiest kids began eating the food. Once Jamie got to know some of the students, he showed them what is in the food they had been eating—chicken nuggets that have mechanically reclaimed meat from bones and skin. The kids were shocked. One said, "So, this is fake food." Jamie then gave them real chicken that he just prepared, and they ate it with delicious pleasure.

> Note what is happening here: The work is harder because people are not yet good at it. As you develop capacity, the work gets easier.

The skinny on "learning is the work" is that it is damn hard, but surprising breakthroughs occur that look easy once they happen. Try making a seemingly simple thing happen across multiple settings, and you soon discover that the simple is complex. But get a few basic things right, combined with resolute leadership and a few skinny ideas up your sleeve, and you can get breakthrough results. From simple to complex and back to simple—pretty astonishing. Complexity loses its mystery.

CHAPTER SEVEN

TRANSPARENCY RULES

Get better at the previous four domains—understanding change itself, mobilizing the power of peers, specializing in capacity building over judgment, and making learning the work—and then trust transparency to do its work. Since the skinny is the naked truth, it is only fitting to realize that transparency must rule.

Transparency is about openness of results in all its subcategories and about what sociologists call *deprivatization of practice*. Why does transparency rule? First, it is almost inevitable these days with the demand for accountability and access to information. As we say, if information is going to get you anyway, you might as well move toward the danger and confront it on an even playing field.

> Transparency is about openness of results in all its subcategories and about what sociologists call *deprivatization of practice*. It is almost inevitable these days with the demand for accountability and access to information.

Second, and more directly to the point, you cannot get system reform without knowing what is being accomplished and who is getting success. Gord Wagner and Jill Maar and their staffs could not pinpoint needed actions unless they knew where every student stood week in and week out in terms of his or her progress. Ontario could not get more schools on the move unless they knew what "on the move" looked like and without easy access to those schools that were getting results.

> There is obviously a strong two-way relationship between transparency and nonjudgmentalism. Let judgment creep into the relationship, and openness recedes.

There is obviously a strong two-way relationship between transparency and nonjudgmentalism. Let judgment creep into the relationship, and openness recedes. To know the skinny here is to know that the main reason for having openness about results and practice is as a *strategy for improvement.* If you get this right, accountability "almost" takes care of itself.

> Assessment for learning prevails in successful schools so that teachers can tailor-make appropriate instruction to individual needs. Practice is transparent so that precision and specificity can be identified and spread.

At the micro (classroom and school) level, motion leaders work to make explicit the two-way causal relationship between instruction and assessment. Assessment for learning prevails in successful schools so that teachers can tailor-make appropriate instruction to individual needs. Practice is transparent so that precision and specificity can be identified and spread.

The mindset at the school level develops in the following sequence, which overlaps in timing. First, schools need to get in the habit of comparing themselves with themselves. How did we do last year, where are we now, where should we be, will we know when we get there, and so on?

Second, schools should seek to compare themselves with other schools facing similar circumstances, in what we call *statistical neighbors*. If others are doing better, we should want to learn how they are doing it. If we are doing better, we need to share. Third, schools should measure their progress against an external standard or benchmark, such as 90% success or how the most successful jurisdictions are faring.

At the macro or system level (districts and states), we have three rules. One, set up a robust, accessible data system—high standards, few in number, and easy and timely accessibility. Two, don't take any one year's results too, too, literally. Think of three-year windows in terms of moving up, down, or flatlined. Three, make it crystal clear that by far the primary role of the data system is for improvement—this means that the first response to underperformance is to invest in capacity building and not to take punitive action.

We have proven that nonpunitive accountability can work in our turnaround schools strategy in Ontario (called Ontario Focused Intervention Partnership—OFIP). In this strategy, all schools that are performing at a low level are identified, along with schools that are stagnant or coasting. About 1,000 of the 4,000 elementary schools have been included. We assume that low performance is a matter of low capacity, and we act accordingly by providing direct help. OFIP schools on the average have improved 10% more than all other schools in the system (all schools in the system have been on the rise). The school that Ben Levin (2008) visited that we talked about in Chapter 3 that went from 20% proficiency in reading to 70% was an OFIP school.

In short, motion leaders prize transparency of results and practice, and prize good help. As we progress (i.e., as relationships and trust get built), we up the ante. We expect progress, and if it is not happening, more overt intervention is called for. Because

> Change-savvy leaders always know that you can't directly *make* people change. But you can create a system where positive change is virtually inevitable.

peers are a big part of the solution, people's colleagues (within schools, within districts, across districts in the state or province) are part and parcel of the pressure scenario. Change-savvy leaders always know that you can't directly *make* people change. But you can create a system where positive change is virtually inevitable. As such, it will look very much like the skinny on change evident in this book.

What if the education world is not this good, and that certain groups might misuse transparent data about performance? The crucial skinny is that you have to take the risk. You have to both trust and get better at transparency. Tim Brighouse knows this when he advises you as leaders to (a) admit that you don't know the answer to a question and commit to finding it, and (b) if something goes wrong in an organization, and you are the leader, take the blame even if it is not your fault (and work on correcting the flaw). If you combine this stance with learning the skinny, you gain more and more respect and more allies. You can afford to be transparent because you become more confident and more powerful. You become more comfortable with what you don't know because you find the future less daunting.

Everybody knows that you learn from mistakes and that you can't learn in a closed system. But experiencing mistakes is an emotionally and politically charged phenomenon. If the leader is not going to break the cycle, who is? Stated another way, practicing transparency is a risk-taking

> Practicing transparency is a risk-taking proposition—no question. But if done well and persistently, the gains far outweigh the costs.

proposition—no question. But if done well and persistently, the gains far outweigh the costs. Motion leaders are prepared to pay the price in order to gain the results. And as they get better at leadership, the cost-benefit ratio tips strongly in their favor.

Being prepared has both a technical and a political dimension. Technically, leaders must become more and more what we call *assessment literate.* They must be able to decipher and use data effectively. They must also be adept at taking this proficiency into the political arena. When parents, the media, and the state want to take issue on a particular matter (if it is a legitimate concern), you need to be Tim Brighouse. But if the data are being used in a distorted, abusing, or unfair manner, the leader must be proactive and articulate in entering the fray and holding firm on what he or she knows. The more the leader becomes assessment literate and the more he or she practices transparency, the better they get at it.

The more the leader becomes assessment literate and the more he or she practices transparency, the better they get at it.

Deprivatizing teaching is a tough one. The history of the teaching profession has been built on the individual professional autonomy of the teacher—what John Goodlad (Goodlad & Klein, 1968) called over forty years ago "behind the classroom door." Today, no profession will thrive that is not willing to measure itself and be open about what it is doing. Every piece of skinny in this book is about cracking the tough nut of deprivatization (not the least of the solutions is our next chapter on love, trust, and resistance). We can go right back to "change itself"—build relationships first and be more challenging second (I have already said that there may be exceptions where leaders have to act early to remove certain derailers, but it is an exception).

Trusting transparency, then, is a skill as well as a stance. Far from being naïve, it is one of the most sophisticated components of leadership. As skills mount, the transparent leader wins just about every time. By contrast, the closed leader loses sooner than later. The world is demanding greater transparency, and technology is accelerating it. The motion leader moves toward the danger and turns it to advantage. Change-savvy leaders become more powerful in so doing. Now, what's love got to do with it?

CHAPTER EIGHT

LOVE, TRUST, AND RESISTANCE

The first of *The Six Secrets of Change* is "love your employees" (Fullan, 2008). When we first developed the workshops on the six secrets, we did it linearly and started with Secret One. But since some employees are clearly not lovable, we got sidetracked. As we further discussed the matter, the most common question was, how do you deal with resistance? Along the way, someone would inevitably declare that trust is everything. Well of course it is, but it begs the question, how do you get trust if you don't have it? It turns out that this trio of love, resistance, and trust are closely interrelated. The skinny is to unravel them and then recombine them with powerful consequences—simplexity once again. Four things:

Do start with love. Some 50 years ago, McGregor (1960) posited Theory X and Theory Y assumptions about people. Theory X assumed a priori that people were inherently lazy, disliked work, and had to be supervised closely. Theory Y said that people would put in the extra effort if the work was meaningful and they were supported by leaders and peers. So make Theory Y your first point of entry. It is not that 100% of people will respond accordingly. Some

There is a central tendency in most people to respond according to how they are treated. And a degree of self-fulfilling prophecy will be at work.

people (for example, because of their internal standards) will do a good job even if they have a Theory X leader, while others will still goof off even if they have a Theory Y boss. The point is that there is a central tendency in most people to respond according to how they are treated. And a degree of self-fulfilling prophecy will be at work. You disadvantage yourself from the outset if you generate the negativity of Theory X or fail to capitalize on the natural energy of Theory Y. Take the chance on Theory Y, and you will gain more than you lose.

Second, trust is powerful, but you must behave your way into it. You must work your way through the natural mistrust that many people have with respect to leaders. There are tons of stories every day that confirm to people that most leaders are out for themselves. You can break trust down into several dimensions, but to me there are just two to remember and model—*integrity* (sincerity, reliability, honesty) and *competence* (skill, effectiveness). Both are important. You don't want to rely on a leader who is 100% sincere but not very competent at what he or she needs to do to lead.

To get over the implementation dip of establishing trust is to be rewarded with what Stephen Covey (the son—2006) calls "the speed of trust." If there is anything worth investing in up front, it is to demonstrate your trustworthiness especially in the face of suspicion or mistrust. This is a huge, powerful investment as Covey says, when you examine the economics of trust. Low trust means low speed (motion slows to a halt) and high cost (financially and emotionally). High trust does the opposite. You can get so much more done, more quickly. The payoff is great. Tony Bryk and Barbara Schneider (2002), in their study of Chicago schools, found that schools reporting high relational trust were three times more likely to improve in reading and mathematics. They also discovered that trust strengthens moral commitment and shared purpose to the point that high-trust schools are more likely to take action in the face of uncaring or persistently ineffective teachers because both the leader and the peers want improvement.

Third, to say trust has high-yield benefits still doesn't say how to get it. To repeat, you have to earn it through demonstrated integrity and competence. The latter two are very much about being change savvy. Thus, every chapter so far identifies skills and practices that add up to becoming more trustworthily effective. The skinny of the skinny is trust—behave your way into it with integrity and competence.

> The skinny of the skinny is trust.

Fourth, what about resistance, per se? Well, as I said above, you can't *make* people change. On the positive side, so many things conspire if you are change savvy that you end up reducing if not eliminating resistance. We have already seen the power of knowing change itself, purposeful peer interaction (which incorporates resisters or makes them increasingly uncomfortable), nonjudgmental capacity building, learning is the work, and transparency of data and practice. These stances and strategies combine to synergize support and pressure as an almost irresistible force.

> Quite often, resisters have a kernel of truth that might be missed if we don't listen and seek different opinions.

"Almost irresistible." There will always be some resistance (and quite often, resisters have a kernel of truth that might be missed if we don't listen and seek different opinions, which is part and parcel of being change savvy anyway). So the idea is

Sir Ernest Shackleton (1874–1922)

to maximize trust and effectiveness in order to reduce resistance to a minimum.

Beyond that, harsh action is sometimes necessary (remember, it is okay to be assertive). In our workshops, we show movie clips from the BBC production about Ernest Shackleton (Fine et al., 2002). Shackleton was an explorer who, 100 years ago, led a crew of 28 men on an expedition to the South Pole. They got halfway there when their ship got choked off by ice formations and destroyed, forcing them to abandon it. Led by Shackleton, they made their way across ice flows and 800 miles of open water in what was no larger than a rowboat. This incredible journey took 18 months.

Many books have been written about Shackleton's leadership qualities because he combined passion, love and care of his men, empathy, problem solving, perseverance, transparency, and clear and realistic communication (he was change savvy, in other words). There is one scene when they are trudging over ice flows ankle deep in freezing, slushy water, dragging the cutter, when a crewmember, Neish, rebels and refuses to go any further—the beginning of mutiny? Shackleton lights into Neish with incredible emotional and articulate ferocity, ending the diatribe with the words, "If you jeopardize the lives of my men I will have no hesitation in having you shot."

It is clear to the viewer that Shackleton was able to get away with such a degree of harshness because he had built up a broad and deep base of mutual respect and trust with the vast majority of the 27 other men. It was his trustworthiness (integrity and competence) that carried the day. When we see Neish go back to the task of moving the cutter across ice, we have little doubt that he was motivated more by the crew's quiet support of their leader than by his fear of being shot. Neish later becomes a committed and valued member of the small rescue team that made it to a whaling station to get help—all 28 men survived.

Shackleton's men welcome him back from his treacherous journey to the whaling station.

Image by Frank Hurley

Sometimes resistance is deeply historically rooted. Recall the story from Chapter 2 about Jonathan Jansen, the first black person to serve as dean of the University of Pretoria in South Africa, appointed in 2000 to create a new intergrated nonracial culture facing down 100 years of all-white traditions.

Jansen's motion leadership savvy is remarkably congruent with the core ideas in this book. Leading cultural change from a minority position in a deeply entrenched institution of more than 40,000 students and 2,000 staff on seven campuses requires all the skinny on change you can muster, including resilient courage. We cannot possibly do justice to the profound cultural upheaval for both blacks and whites in those seven years (read Jansen's heart- and mind-moving account in *Knowledge in the Blood* [2009a]).

In a briefer treatment, Jansen reflects on and identifies seven themes that underpinned the skinny of change for his leadership:

1. We must reorganize the politics of emotions that energize behaviors.
2. The change strategy cannot create victims.
3. The problem must be named and confronted.
4. Leaders must exemplify the expected standards of behavior.
5. We must engage emotionally with students in their world.
6. Teachers and principals themselves are sometimes actors.
7. The environment must accommodate risk. (Jansen, 2009b, p. 189)

Jonathan Jansen, Dean of Education, University of Pretoria (2001–2007), combating 100 years of tradition

Consider the dilemmas in the following two situations Jonathan handled:

> In the case of the lecturer who intersperses her teaching with snide racial comments about the capabilities of black students, a leader must make it clear that racism is unacceptable, that a higher standard of behavior is

required, and that the continuation of racial insult will lead to dismissal. The confrontation is not about the lecturer per se; it is about broader communication to the watchful audience of campus dwellers and surrounding communities for whom taking a stand is an indication of what is acceptable and what is not; and of the position of leadership on this potentially explosive issue. (Jansen, 2009b, p. 240)

At the same time, Jansen is able to empathize with

. . . Max, a teacher of South African history for more than 25 years. As a white South African reared in the political vortex of the apartheid years, Max came to understand deeply that the history of white settlement was one of triumph over adversity, of civilization over backwardness, of Calvinist faith against atheistic communism, of freedom against tyranny. He lost members of his family in the border wars, witnessed the struggle of his parents against white poverty, and then the gradual rise, through the discipline of hard work, to a comfortable though not extravagant middle-class lifestyle. Then Nelson Mandela was elected in 1994, and a new history was suddenly to be taught with different narrative from the ones he had come to believe and thus relied upon to make his choices in life. For him, the teaching of history is emotional knowledge, even though he accepts, in his mind, the inevitability of a new official knowledge. (p. 243)

Here is Jansen at once confronting, empathetic, role model, communicator of the new regime, and action man. He knows about the politics and emotions of integrating the firm handling of resistance with building trust, respect, and, eventually, mutual allegiance.

> Learn to combine love, trustworthiness, and empathetic but firm handling of resistance, and you will be rewarded by the speed of change. Complex becomes simply powerful.

In short, handling resistance and building relationships are part and parcel of the same strategy. Skinny change agents work on the most difficult relationships in order to turn them into a force for positive movement. When this is done well, even the most intransigent situations can be overcome in fairly short time frames. With change savvy, the complex becomes manageable.

CHAPTER NINE

LEADERSHIP FOR ALL

The paradox about becoming change savvy is that it makes you more confident and humble at the same time. In this respect, leaders have two responsibilities: to be always learning and refining the skinny of change and to realize that they have an equal responsibility to teach others the same. Leaders developing leaders multiply their effects.

> Becoming change savvy makes you more confident and humble at the same time. In this respect, leaders have two responsibilities: to be always learning and refining the skinny of change and to realize that they have an equal responsibility to teach others the same.

Everyone knows that the future is inherently unpredictable. Motion leaders not only learn so much about the essence of change but also become comfortable, even excited, about heading into the next change situation. They exude what we have come to call "more confidence than the situation seems to warrant." Every piece of knowledge and skill we have been discussing in the previous chapters has come from reflective experience. These leaders really do know a hell of a lot. They don't find complexity complex. People do expect their leaders to help them find the way, to find hope no matter what. By taking the mystery out of complexity, they reassure people that progress is probable.

Where does humility fit in? Back to the definition of *wisdom*—using your knowledge while doubting what you know. Motion leaders are learners; they are not know-it-alls. They are experts in change, which means that they are much quicker to read a situation and know what to do, and they are much more adept at learning. They become confident that they and others can figure it out because this capacity is virtually built into change savvy.

There is certainly an element of spirituality or moral purpose in the equation. The values embedded in respecting and wanting change—integrity, respect for and faith in others, commitment to bringing humankind to a higher level of accomplishment, and even appreciating that individuals and groups are not perfect—all have a moral base. Resolute leadership is morally driven, but it is also change-savvy driven. It is as if the change is so important morally that figuring out how to enact it is equally crucial. Motion leadership gives moral purpose wheels and wings.

Resolute leadership is morally driven, but it is also change-savvy driven. Motion leadership gives moral purpose wheels and wings.

There has been more written about leadership in the literature on organizations than any other topic, and there are no signs that it is abating. I can't say that the literature is gaining on clarity. It seems more of a case of striving for complexity and achieving clutter.

It is true that some of the recent leadership development approaches are better because they are *job-embedded.* They place individuals in real settings for longer periods under the guidance of a mentor. But let's look more closely. Such programs respect context. They embrace the old adage that context is everything.

> Motion leadership *changes context* for the very reason that context *is* everything.

Motion leadership is different. It *changes context* for the very reason that context *is* everything. Change savvy is about how to move individuals, organizations, and systems. In short, it is about changing context for the better. Motion leaders need to be explicitly aware that this is the business they are in.

Motion leaders change context because they change other leaders around them who in turn change each other. You can see this in York Region when literally thousands of change leaders have redefined the context, the very system within which they work (Sharratt & Fullan, 2009). You can see it vividly in NorthWest 3 (NW3), the family of schools in one of the most challenging high-poverty areas within the Toronto District School Board with 18 schools and some 11,000 students. When you listen to Gen Ling Chang, the superintendent of the group, describe in very specific terms the network strategy of focusing and networking groups to build capacity, you can't help but be impressed. And when you hear principal after principal, literacy coach after literacy coach, and teacher after teacher describe the actions and the outcomes, you become a true believer. The words come tripping off literacy coach Sucheta Jones's tongue as she talks about how she feels part of the whole network compared to all those years of toiling away by herself; and instead of people doing their own thing for so many years, they now have the same focused goals, the same language; and how when you listen to everyday teachers, they sound like instructional leaders (Ontario Literacy Numeracy Secretariat, 2008).

No wonder it pays off. In four years, 2004–2008, reading proficiency scores across all elementary schools in NorthWest 3 have risen from 59% to 70% in Grade 3, and from 65% to 79% in Grade 6.

The same for writing—61% to 71% and 59% to 71% in Grades 3 and 6, respectively. A system of leaders has dramatically changed their context.

In *Motion Leadership the Movie* (MLM), you will see practitioners displaying and talking about how to change context, that is, how to get movement. When leaders can clearly and succinctly articulate what they are doing, show results, and explain exactly how they got them, you know that they have the skinny. When a lot of leaders do this simultaneously and they cultivate it in others, it becomes a revolution. When you become part of the movie, we begin to see real change on a scale never before seen.

The skinny-savvy emperor or empress self-consciously wears no clothes. But they don't strut their stuff. They are humble with what they have been given, and they make more than the best of it.

The skinny on change is to unclutter it—to strip away the fat to a very small number of gems that have the virtue of being simultaneously simple and powerful. The skinny-savvy emperor or empress self-consciously wears no clothes. But they don't strut their stuff. They are humble with what they have been given, and they make more than the best of it. Motion leadership makes everybody look good. What could be more exciting than that?

Let's leave the last word to Nora. At the end of her journey, having helped change the eating habits of the vast majority of 20,000 children, she says, "It is funny how you can change, however old you are." The magic of change savvy!

REFERENCES

Boyle, A. (2009). *Tower Hamlets case story.* Unpublished paper. Beyond Expectations Project, Boston College.

Bryk, A., & Schneider, B. (2002). *Trust in schools.* New York: Russell Sage.

City, E., Elmore, R., Fiarman, S., & Teitel, L. (2009). *Instructional rounds in education.* Cambridge, MA: Harvard Education Press.

Cole, P. (2004). *Professional development: A great way to avoid change.* Melbourne, Australia: Centre for Strategic Education.

Covey, S. M. R. (2006). *The speed of trust.* New York: Free Press.

Dufour, R., Dufour, R., Eaker, R., & Karhanek, G. (2010). *Raising the bar and closing the gap: Whatever it takes.* Bloomington, IN: Solution Tree Press.

Fine, D., Nunez, E., Barra, F., Ryle-Hodges, R., Roberts, S. (Producers), & Sturridge, C. (Writer/Director). (2002). *Shackleton: The greatest survival story of all time* [Motion Picture]. UK: BBC.

Fullan, M. (2008). *The six secrets of change.* San Francisco: Jossey-Bass.

Fullan, M. (2010). *All systems go.* Thousand Oaks, CA: Corwin.

Gittell, J. (2003). *The Southwest Airlines way.* New York: McGraw-Hill.

Gladwell, M. (2009). *Outliers: The story of success.* New York: Little, Brown.

Goodlad, J., & Klein, F. (1968). *Looking behind the classroom door.* Mahwah, NJ: Lawrence Erlbaum.

Herold, D., & Fedor, D. (2008). *Change the way you lead change.* Palo Alto, CA: Stanford University Press.

Jansen, J. (2009a). *Knowledge in the blood.* Palo Alto, CA: Stanford University Press.

Jansen, J. (2009b). When politics and emotion meet: Educational change in radically divided communities. In A. Hargreaves & M. Fullan (Eds.), *Change wars* (pp. 185–200). Bloomington, IN: Solution Tree.

Kluger, J. (2008). *Simplexity.* New York: Hyperion Books.

Levin, B. (2008). *How to change 5000 schools.* Cambridge, MA: Harvard Education Press.

Liker, J., & Hoseus, M. (2008). *Toyota culture: The heart and soul of the Toyota way.* New York: McGraw-Hill.

Liker, J., & Meier, D. (2007). *The Toyota way.* New York: McGraw-Hill.

May, M. (2009). *In pursuit of elegance: When the best ideas have something missing.* New York: Broadway Books.

McGregor, D. (1960). *The human side of enterprise.* New York: McGraw-Hill.

McGuinty, D. (2009, June 30). *Lessons learned.* Speech given at the Global Education Competiveness Summit, Washington, DC.

Mintzberg, H. (2004). *Managers not MBAs.* San Francisco: Berrett-Koehler.

Mortenson, G., & Relin, O. (2009). *Three cups of tea.* New York: Penguin Books.

Oliver, J. (2009). *Jamie's school dinners.* Freemantle Media [DVD]. Available from http://www.jamieoliver.com/dvd/school-dinners-dvd.

Ontario Literacy Numeracy Secretariat. (2008). *Networked learning communities* [DVD collection]. Toronto, ON: Author.

Peters, T., & Waterman, R. (1982). *In search of excellence.* New York: HarperCollins.

Pfeffer, J., & Sutton, R. (2008). *Hard facts, dangerous half-truths and total nonsense.* Boston: Harvard Business School Press.

Reeves, D. (2009). *Leading change in your school.* Alexandria, VA: Association of School Curriculum Development.

Robinson, V. M. J., Lloyd, C., & Rowe, K. J. (2008). The impact of leadership on student outcomes: An analysis of the differential effects of leadership type. *Educational Administration Quarterly, 44*(5), 635–674.

Sharratt, L., & Fullan, M. (2009). *Realization.* Thousand Oaks, CA: Corwin.

Taylor, W., & LaBarre, P. (2006). *Mavericks at work.* New York: Morrow.

York Region District School Board. (2007). *Jersey elementary school* [DVD]. Aurora, ON: Author. Available from York Region District School Board, The Education Centre, 60 Wellington Street West, Box 40, Aurora, ON L4G 3H2.

INDEX

CORWIN
A SAGE Company

The Corwin logo—a raven striding across an open book—represents the union of courage and learning. Corwin is committed to improving education for all learners by publishing books and other professional development resources for those serving the field of PreK–12 education. By providing practical, hands-on materials, Corwin continues to carry out the promise of its motto: **"Helping Educators Do Their Work Better."**

OPC
ONTARIO
PRINCIPALS'
COUNCIL

The Ontario Principals' Council (OPC) is a voluntary professional association for principals and vice-principals in Ontario's public school system. We believe that exemplary leadership results in outstanding schools and improved student achievement. To this end, we foster quality leadership through world-class professional services and supports. As an ISO 9001 registered organization, we are committed to our statement that "quality leadership is our principal product."